Survivors
Lost

John Goodwin

Published in association with
The Basic Skills Agency

Hodder Murray
A MEMBER OF THE HODDER HEADLINE GROUP

Orders: please contact Bookpoint Ltd, 130 Milton Park, Abingdon, Oxon OX14 4SB. Telephone: (44) 01235 827720. Fax: (44) 01235 400454. Lines are open 9.00–6.00, Monday to Saturday, with a 24-hour message answering service. Visit our website at www.hoddereducation.co.uk

© John Goodwin 2005
First published in 2005 by
Hodder Murray, a member of the Hodder Headline Group
338 Euston Road
London NW1 3BH

Impression number   10 9 8 7 6 5 4 3 2
Year   2010 2009 2008 2007 2006 2005

All rights reserved. Apart from any permitted use under UK copyright law, no part of this publication may be reproduced or transmitted in any form or by any means, electronic or mechanical, including photocopy, recording, or any information, storage and retrieval system, without permission in writing from the publisher or under licence from the Copyright Licensing Agency Limited. Further details of such licences (for reprographic reproduction) may be obtained from the Copyright Licensing Agency Limited, of 90 Tottenham Court Road, London W1T 4LP.

Cover photo © Jon Sparks/Alamy.
Illustrations by Gary Andrews.
Typeset by Transet Limited, Coventry, England.
Printed in Great Britain by Athenaeum Press Ltd, Gateshead, Tyne & Wear.

A catalogue record for this title is available from the British Library

ISBN-10: 0 340 90070 9
ISBN-13: 978 0 340 90070 3

About the Play

The People
- Ben — the group leader
- Harry — his friend
- Jez — a loudmouth
- Lucy — his friend
- Tariq — the serious one
- Watson — their instructor

What's Happening
The characters in the play are on a Survivors' Big Challenge Walk.

Act 1

The group are walking on the moors.
They are lost in thick fog.

Jez	We're lost.
Ben	No, we're not.
Tariq	We should go back.
Jez	There's no path to get us back.
Lucy	The fog's so thick.
	I can't see anything.
Tariq	Scary.
Harry	My compass says
	we should go this way.
Jez	Stuff your compass.
Ben	Come on.
	Cut out the arguing.
Jez	We've been walking all day.
	I'm not going any further.
Lucy	Nor am I.

They both sit down.

Ben   We can't stop here.
Jez   Why not?
Ben   It will be dark soon.
         We have to get to the campsite.
Jez   Watson shouldn't have made us hand in our mobiles.
Harry   We need to use the compass.
Jez   I'm not moving.
Ben   Now you're being stupid.
Jez   We should open the black box.
Tariq   Yeah. And use the mobile inside it.
Ben   That's only for an emergency.
Lucy   This *is* an emergency.
Harry   Watson will kill us if we open that.
Ben   If we open the box,
         we've lost the challenge.
Jez   I don't care about the stupid challenge.
         It was pathetic anyway …

Lucy	I've got a blister on my toe from all this walking.
Ben	We can't give up now.
Jez	Well, we have.
Lucy	I just want a hot shower.
Ben	You can have a shower at the campsite.
Jez	Come on, open the box.
Harry	The fog is clearing.
Jez	If you don't open that box, Ben, I will. Right?
Harry	I can see the river. Look.
Ben	Grow up, Jez.
Harry	And the campsite is there. Right by the river. Look down there.
Tariq	Yeah, I can see it.
Ben	Well spotted. Just a bit further.

	Then you can step

                Then you can step
right into that hot shower, Lucy.

Lucy How far is it?

Ben Come on.
Let's get down there.

Jez I told you, I'm not moving.

Ben You up for it, Harry?

Harry Yeah.

Ben Tariq?

Tariq Yeah.

Ben What about you, Lucy?

Lucy Don't know yet.

Ben Well, we're going on.
I've got the black box
in my rucksack.
You two can please yourselves.

Lucy Hang about.
Wait for me.

Ben Catch us up.

Harry What shall we do about Jez?

Ben He'll follow us.

Tariq You sure?

Ben, **Tariq** *and* **Harry** *walk off.*
Lucy *hops after them.*
Jez *looks down at the ground.*

Act 2

At the campsite.
Ben *is cooking beans.*

Tariq   Nearly dark.
Ben   The beans are ready.
Tariq   Where's Jez?
Lucy   He'll be here in a minute.
Tariq   You said that an hour ago.
    He must have got lost.
Harry   I'm starving.
Tariq   We should go and look for him.
    Anything could have happened.
Ben   I love cooking beans.
Tariq   People die on those moors.
    You're the leader, Ben.
    You should go and look for him.
Ben   Jez is not lost, Tariq.
Tariq   How do you know?

Ben   I know Jez and his tricks.
Tariq   What tricks?
Harry   Are we going to eat the beans now?

A truck comes into the campsite.

Lucy   What's that doing here?
Ben   Maybe Watson's checking up on us.

The truck door opens.
The truck drives off.

Harry   That's not Watson's motor.
Jez   Hi, guys.
Ben   Did you get a lift in that truck?
Jez   I can smell beans.
Ben   Getting a lift is against the rules.
Jez   Got any burgers as well?
Ben   Get your hands off those beans.
Jez   Don't you …

Ben *pulls the bean pan away from* **Jez**.
It tips over.
All the beans fall on the grass.

Harry   Oh no.

Watson *walks into the campsite.*

Watson   You all found the campite, then.
                The first day of your challenge
                is done.
                But tomorrow is harder.
Tariq   Harder?
Watson   Yes, Tariq. Harder.
Tariq   Oh no.
Watson   You have to find your way
                to White Edge Rock
                by one o'clock.
                It's marked on your map.
                Then you all have to climb
                the rock.
                The whole group.
Harry   We'll never do that.
Watson   Yes, you will.
                I'll see you tomorrow.
                Ben …
Ben   Yes?

Watson	Can you clean up these beans?
	We want to keep things tidy.
Ben	What?
Watson	You all seem
	to be getting on so well.
	See you tomorrow.

Watson *goes. Everyone stares at* **Jez**.

Act 3

At the campsite.
Later that night.
Jez *and* **Lucy** *are standing outside a tent.*
The rest of the group are asleep inside the tent.

Jez　　　　I've had enough.
Lucy　　　 I know what you mean.
Jez　　　　I'm ready to pack it in.
Lucy　　　 I could eat a bag of chips.
Jez　　　　And a burger.
Lucy　　　 With a salad.
Jez　　　　And gravy.
Lucy　　　 Gravy?
Jez　　　　I love gravy with everything.
　　　　　　 Thick brown gravy.

Lucy	I could do
	with a good night's sleep.
	In my own bed.
	I'd sleep all day.
	Not get up at all.
Jez	Let's get out now.
Lucy	Oh yeah.
Jez	Come on.
	We can do it.
Lucy	How?
Jez	We nick the mobile.
	Phone for a taxi.
Lucy	No chance.
Jez	We've just got to get
	that black box.
Lucy	Ben has it in his rucksack.
Jez	So?
Lucy	His rucksack is his pillow.
	It's right under his head.
	You've got no chance.
Jez	We've got every chance.
Lucy	Dream on, Jez.

Jez	I'm going to the back of the tent.
Lucy	What for?
Jez	You wait here.
Lucy	What are you on about?
Jez	We both pull the tent poles out. Then the tent will collapse.
Lucy	So?
Jez	Then you scream as loud as you can. They'll all be in a panic.
Lucy	What?
Jez	I'll nip in and get the box.
Lucy	It'll never work.
Jez	It will be pitch black in the tent. They won't be able to see a thing. Ready?
Lucy	I don't know.
Jez	Just do it, Lucy.

Jez goes to the back of the tent.

Jez Now!

They pull out the poles.

Jez Scream, Lucy.
Scream!

Lucy *screams.*
The tent collapses.

Act 4

Inside the collapsed tent.
It is pitch black.
Tariq *and* **Harry** *are in a panic.*
They speak quickly.

Tariq	Who's that?
Harry	Who screamed?
Tariq	The tent's collapsed.
Harry	What's going on?
Tariq	I tell you the tent's collapsed.
Harry	I can't see anything.
Ben	Keep calm.
Harry	Who's that?
Tariq	Is that you, Harry?
Ben	Got you.
Tariq	What's going on?
Ben	I knew it was you.
Jez	Get off me.

Harry	Get out of the tent.
Tariq	Get out.

They all get out of the tent.
Ben *has* **Jez** *in an arm lock.*

Jez	Get off me.
Ben	I knew it was you.
Jez	Get your hands off me.
Ben	He was trying to get the mobile.
Jez	No, I wasn't.
Ben	I heard you planning it.
Jez	I wasn't.
Ben	You and Lucy. Out here. Isn't that right, Lucy?
Lucy	It was all his idea.
Ben	They pulled the tent down.
Jez	I'm going to get you, Ben.
Ben	You're pathetic.
Jez	Before this is done. I'll get you. I swear I will.

Act 5

The next day at the White Edge Rock.

Watson This is the final challenge.
You have to climb the rock.
And abseil down it.
As simple as that.
Tariq It doesn't look simple.
Watson It's not as bad as it looks.
Tariq It's high.
Watson Not that high.
Tariq And sheer.
Harry I can't see any handholds.
Or footholds.
Watson I'll climb it first.
You can watch
where I put my feet and hands.

Watson *starts to climb.*

Watson	I told you it wasn't too hard.
Tariq	It still looks hard to me.
Harry	He'll soon be at the top.
Lucy	He makes everything look easy.
Harry	He's climbed it.

Watson *shouts down from the top of the rock.*

Watson	Now I'm going to abseil down.

Watson *comes down in an abseil.*

	Excellent.
	You can climb it next, Ben.
	I'll fix a safety rope first.
	Then you can climb.
	Pass me the rope, Jez.
Jez	This rope?
Watson	Yes, that's the one.
Jez	Right.

Watson *fixes the safety rope.*

Watson	Good.
	Now up you go, Ben.

Ben *begins to climb.*

Ben	It's hard.
Watson	Don't worry.
	If you slip,
	the safety rope will hold you.
	Just relax.
Harry	(*shouting*) Stop!
	Something's wrong
	with the safety rope.
	Look.
	It's been cut with a knife.
Watson	I can't see anything.
Harry	Look closer.
	Look there.
	See that cut?
Watson	I can see it now.
	A cut halfway through the rope.

Tariq   Jez was messing about
              with that rope.
              That was back at the camp.
Watson   What did you do to the rope, Jez?

Jez *is silent.*

Watson   I asked you what you did to the rope.

Jez *is still silent.*

Watson   You could have killed someone.
Harry   He said he'd get Ben.
              He swore he would.
Lucy   He wanted to stop the challenge.
Tariq   He wanted to ruin it.
Watson   Is that right?

Jez *is still silent.*

Watson	This is a matter for the police. You and I will be going to see them. Right now, Jez. You'll have to climb down, Ben.
Ben	What?
Watson	Come down. The challenge is over.
Ben	But that means Jez has won.
Harry	That's just what he wanted to happen.
Ben	Can't we go on? Use another safety rope?
Harry	We've come all this way.
Tariq	Walked for ages.
Lucy	And got blisters.
Harry	Had our dinner tipped in the grass.
Tariq	Got lost in the fog.
Watson	But if you've had such a bad time, why do you want to finish it?
Ben	Because we do.

Harry	We can't give up.
Lucy	Not now.
Tariq	Let's go for it.
Ben	We don't want to be losers after all this.
Watson	All right. I've got another safety rope in my car. You can do the climb and the abseil.
Lucy	Can we have a party?
Watson	A party?
Lucy	If we do the challenge?
Watson	Maybe.
Lucy	Not 'maybe' please, Watson. Just say yes.
Watson	Oh, all right. Yes.

Ben, **Tariq**, **Lucy** *and* **Harry** *cheer.*
Jez *is silent.*